Man on Terrace with Wine

Man on Terrace with Wine

Poems by

Miles David Moore

Cover design by Shay Culligan

ISBN: 978-1-952326-66-0

Kelsay Books
502 South 1040 East, A-119
American Fork, Utah, 84003

To my sister Stephanie—
as always, my best audience

Acknowledgments

The poems in this book have been published or are scheduled to be published in the following journals and anthologies:

Innisfree Poetry Journal: "The Blessing of Peacocks," "Emoticon," "A Taste to Die For," "The Man Who Hated Oceans," "Italian-American," "Poetry and Music," "Shadow Dancing," "Warning," "Glove Puppet," "A Lesson from a Tooth," "Nothing Stops."

The Broadkill Review: "Turtle Meat," "The Horse"

Bogg: "Early Flowers"

Passager: "Ships and Barges"

Poetic Voices Without Borders 2: "The Good Fight"

Minimus: "Chain Letter"

Gargoyle: "Autumn Directive," "Lines Written on an Intercity Bus," "A Soaking Rain," "Grandma and the Hurricane," "Doe at a Street Corner," "His Face," "To an Obscure Vegetable," "Man on Terrace with Wine, Recalling a Line from Hermann Hesse"

Beltway Poetry Quarterly: "Danse d'Enfer," "Watching Godzilla in 3D"

Arlington Literary Journal (ArLiJo): "Hopper: *Cape Cod Evening,*" "It Was Over So Fast," "Poem of Ecstasy"

Pale House: "The Afterlife of Adolf Hitler," "Elvis and Di's Nuptials in Heaven"

WordWrights!: "A Mother Waits," "Grotesque," "Alan Arkin Wins the Steak Knives"

Measure: "A Vandalized Churchyard," "Nursery Rhyme"

Heliotrope: "Cornflowers"

BigCityLit.com: "To Avoid Paris," "The King's Return"

Light: "To a Modern Poet," "Drink Up"

Rattapallax: "Death of a Barber"

The Poet's Quest for God: "A Modern Nativity"

A Sea of Alone: Poems for Alfred Hitchcock: "*Shadow of a Doubt:* Charles Oakley's Speech"

"Early Flowers" was a winner of the Moving Words competition sponsored by the Washington Metropolitan Transit Authority and the Arlington Arts Council.

"Alan Arkin Wins the Steak Knives" was reprinted in *Carquinez Poetry Review.*

"Ships and Barges" and "Italian-American" were reprinted in *Arlington Literary Review (ArLiJo).*

"Hopper: *Cape Cod Evening*" is scheduled to be reprinted in *Written in Arlington* (Paycock Press, edited by Katherine E. Young).

Contents

I. What Serves You Right

The Blessing of Peacocks

for Hilary Tham

It was dusk at St. Mary's; the last of the light
whispered down lawns that sloped to the inlet.
You were parking your van with the Chinese horses
rampant where you painted them on the hood
when, square on the grass in front of us,
a peacock fanned in full his courtship feathers
of lime, teal, coral, lapis lazuli.

I joked I didn't realize your van
resembled a peahen so lusciously.
But this is what I've always wished for you:
the unexpected blessings of jeweled nature,
pure scenes of grace that take the form of flowers
bowing before you, or the dance of birds
in tribute to one who makes things beautiful.

Early Flowers

Forsythia bear a hanging blight, a wilt
like clowns on gallows. Frost-blasted daffodils

crumple, brown sunspots of cancerous bloom.
They were lured by a false warmth in February

to believe in April. Trusting their senses
to spring, they cast away their infant wool

and opened their petals to a lion's embrace.

Turtle Meat

Ohio, 1963

Turtle fishermen wade to their waists
in turbid creeks, a feast for leeches.
Sticking gloved hands under rocks and logs,
they pray the snapping ends aren't facing forward.
But they get five bucks a pound for turtle—
big money for men with wives, kids, two jobs.

Poured from the canvas sack,
the olive-drab turtles tumble,
their slow eyes blinking at the backyard sun,
their prehistoric claws raking the grass.
Those who roll over on their bowler backs
will be righted to spend their final seconds
crawling too slowly away.

The men's lips work cigarettes,
ash and sparks raining on turtle heads
severed with three or four smooth-bladed cuts
to wattled necks. The earth marinates
in the rotting-iron stench of blood.
Hammers splinter shells, knives lay open
unprotected hearts still needlessly beating.

All the children who benefit
from turtles dismembered, who watch behind
corners to peek from and fingers that splay
from horrified eyes, who whisper a chant
of "I hate turtle, I won't eat it,"
will sample the end on a Melmac plate:
turtle parts left over from the sale
to richer folk—knobby, angular,
fried to a Sunday brown, and tasting
like the darkest meat of chicken.

Emoticon

Colon-right parenthesis smiley face
appended sideways to an e-mail's end,
you carry on your nonexistent back
the weight of every writer's good intentions.
You are the Irony Accessory—
the tacked-on laugh, the shrug, the raised eyebrow
to show the humor in what reads on screen
as a punch in the face. The modulating warmth
of a human voice or a human hand's
scrawl upon paper, read in warm lamplight,
is lost in the computer's literal glare.
You are the fall guy, the "Kick Me" sign
stuck on a sentence's butt, so when
someone *does* want to kick you—
and believe me, someone will—
your changeless smile shows your good grace
in accepting what serves you right. ☺

A Taste to Die For

The Americans love Pepsi-Cola. We love death.
—Afghan Mujahedeen commander
quoted in the Daily Telegraph,
October 2001

The first sip gives you pause.
Rich, mineral, like molten rubies,
the flavor carries notes of chocolate,
apples, black pepper, asparagus, tarragon—
everything that you have ever tasted.
The bouquet is of roses, smoke, mown grass,
rain on a spring morning, the head of a lover
soft and yielding against a down pillow.

The finish is surprisingly short.
That taste—even more surprisingly—
comes not from the lips, but up from the throat.
The man who took aim at you thinks he knows
the things he loves, and the things you love.
He expects brown syrup to fizz
from your inhuman veins, and your alien world
to shatter like glass, crumple like aluminum,
or melt like plastic.

The Man Who Hated Oceans

They were too big for his blood.
He walked alongside them, resenting
the grit and shell-shards stabbing his feet,
the waves that first kissed then slapped the shore,
the stink of dead fish, the animal roar
of vast, undrinkable amorphousness.
He saw absolutely nothing remarkable
about Tinkertoy freighters in the pinpoint distance
or Ken-doll surfers in their death-wish curl.
Staring at calm seas from a balcony
or the turbulent heights of a jet,
he thought them a sop to the cult of romance,
a mirror for the world's self-regard.

He preferred rivers—or, more accurately, creeks.
He loved—no, not loved; felt comfortable with
the damming of waters in narrow ditches.
Creeks flowed serenely in subdued confinement,
and when they jumped their banks, everyone agreed
they were wrong and bad. They could be diverted
for anybody's purposes, even his.
This validation buoyed his soul until,
at last, he found his own narrow ditch.

Ships and Barges

Some wreck themselves on the rocks
or, more perversely, against each other,
drowning all that swims or flies
in the smothering darkness of their poison.
Some, with Damn-the-Torpedoes courage,
sail into Force Five hurricanes,
and all that survives is synecdoche
of flotsam, jetsam, caps and shoes.
Some dock at home in a hero's flourish
of flags and trumpets, the people cheering
the brigands who will rob them blind
in the flash-toothed sale of cargo holds
engorged with zircons and mica.

Then there are the quiet ones,
weighted with coal and bread and wood
till their gunwales are nearly flush with the waves.
In daylight, their rust spots fester;
at night, their lights are faint
even to those who would die without them.

An Angel in Winter

She is folding in upon herself,
a frost-tinged flower, her legs as frail
as dandelion stems. Sleeping
sixteen hours out of twenty-four,
she is a translucent spirit,
all time the same to her.

Sometimes she wakes
with newborn eyes on an alien world.
"What's wrong, Mom? Did you have a dream?"
Her voice comes slowly, softly. "Honey,
I feel I've been touched by the hand of God."

The Horse

Barely a yearling, the horse
parts the high grass to meet us at the fence
that separates the meadow from the graveyard.
Snuffling the wire mesh, he waits
patiently for us to admire him
and stroke his palomino muzzle.

We, who have just left the ashes
of husband, father, grandfather,
are weary of farewells, and turn slowly away.
When we leave the horse, he whinnies—
a sound as lonely as a winter midnight.

Two months later, I return
to mown grass, a distant house and cows.
The flags on the graves snap like whips
in the wind that canters along the fence
and nickers in the trees.

The Good Fight

The English Channel surged below you,
its waves licking American bones.
It was D-Day Plus Fifty, Utah Beach,
and all five-foot-three of you
with a thousand other nurses, helmeted,
full-field-packed, clambered down
the rope ladders swaying against the ship.
The transports were like children's toys
bobbing below. *Don't look down,*
don't slip, your commanders told you.
Your pack will drag you straight to the bottom.
The Norman fields boomed in the distance
as the waves moaned their hunger.

Sixty summers distant from France,
the explosion was in your brain.
You take lessons on how to lace a shoe,
how to walk with a cane.
Your voice, musical as always,
lilts over the nursing center's phone:
Honey, I'm going home today.
Could you please call my mom and dad
and tell them to come get me?

Mother, you climb a ladder now.
The sky is hazy above you,
a fog of dreams and memories.
The decades are your backpack now.
Please don't look down. Please don't slip.
You fight the good fight, now as then.

Mao Laughed

at the child acrobat in Shanghai
who slipped on her final vault and fell
twenty feet to the stage.

All the good Party members froze,
not only at the sight of the motionless child,
but the thought at what else, and how often,
Mao would laugh.

Autumn Directive

Take a handful of fallen leaves.
Write a different message on each.
Make sure the messages make no sense,
even to yourself.
Make sure they contradict each other.
Make sure at least half of them call for blood.
Make sure that the more beautiful the leaf,
the more implacable the message.

Then let the leaves all blow away.
Later, after the snow has fallen,
dream of the leaves decayed to compost,
their ink poisoning the earth.

Warning

Step away, sir.
That doesn't belong to you.
We know it is beautiful, sir,
but what makes you think you have a right to look?

Yes, we see how it shines, sir,
but if you were worthy of it,
you'd see it *more* than shines.
A hundred million golden suns
above the Grand Canyon, the Valley of the Kings,
the Luxembourg Gardens and Diamond Head,
shaded and framed by sequoias and roses,
first kisses and the laughter of blameless children
don't have the patina of this.

That's why we must protect it, sir.
We're always on guard for the likes of you.
The look on your shifty, ungrateful face
tells us the lowdown place you come from:
no kings, no gardens, no blameless children.

We won't tell you twice, sir.
Do we have to use our Tasers?
The ropes that tie the pylons together
loop just as easily around a neck.

There, sir, the owners are coming to claim it.
See how they laugh. See how they kiss.
Walk away, sir, as fast and far as you can.
Show's over. Don't make us do our duty.

And step away from that mirror too, sir.
Nothing to see there.

Glove Puppet

Go limp.
Hollow yourself out.
Retain no speck of skin or sweat
through which a hunter's hound can trace you.
Wear the motley they choose for you
with nothing so great as pride, but be
the eternal, toothless, smiling face.
Or, if you must have teeth, make sure
they're of the same soft felt as you.
Even the gentlest omega wolf
has fangs to justify a bullet.

They have you where they think they want you:
their arms your backbone, their fists your brain.
The fleshly crowd contorts in laughter,
never realizing they've sat on those arms
throughout the ages, or knowing
those programmed fingers move their mouths.

At least with you, from time to time,
the arms grow tired and remove themselves.
You are alone, left wherever
they lay you, but free.
The hearth fire, meaning warmth to some
and the reek of roasting flesh to others,
paints with its light on darkened walls,
revealing to you and only you
the glow of something beautiful.

Grotesque

Because you despise
me, I have become
a pillar. I support
Hell's ceiling with
a billion brothers
and sisters. The
sulfurous fires
baste us, melting
away our adipose
tissue so grease
sweats from our
pores. Our crisp
brown skins shine
like dried blood.
Our clothes burned
off eons ago. Our bones
decalcify, our flesh
hangs and grows slack,
our shoulders hump.
Call us Atlas, call
us Quasimodo. We
hunch in the flame
for you, for all the
tourists who come
to laugh at the funny
dead. We stare with
emptied eyes, we speak
with mouths twisted
ape-open to say
you will never
leave, you who are
no better than us.

Chain Letter

This is not an Irish blessing.
It contains no ancient Navajo wisdom.
The Pope and the Dalai Lama haven't seen this
and wouldn't care if they did.
If you ignore this, you will die eventually.
If you send it on, you will die eventually.
If you read it, you may win the lottery,
though reading it won't help your chances.
You'll have a better chance of being killed by lightning,
though that probably won't happen either.

You may die today or in seventy years,
but, however long you live, it will be *your* life.
You may not find lasting love.
You may be a Casanova
or a celibate Emily Dickinson.
You may get that big promotion
or end up sleeping on steam grates.
You may or may not be accused of a crime.
You may or may not commit a crime.
You may have that magic idea
that will have schoolchildren singing your name
throughout the reverent centuries.
You *will* make friends without quite knowing how
and enemies without quite knowing how.

It's entirely up to you
whether you make a paper airplane
with this, lay it down to train your puppy,
start fires with it or pass it on
to no one or to everyone alive.
But, whatever you do, you will not break the chain.
You are incapable of breaking the chain.

Like everyone who reads or doesn't read this,
you will stare at a nondescript blob of face
decaying in glass. You will wonder at the cage
of flesh that imprisons you, the name
everyone mouths as if it were the sum
of you, the tyranny of tastes,
opinions, and pronouncements known as you.
You may or may not be able to bear it
when the democratic ax-man smashes the cage
and a hundred thousand million fractured atoms
form the same chain, another, or none.

At the Very End

that you should die happy
and prosperous, or, barring that,
happy with little, or else
content with little. Or, should it be your lot
to have nothing, that you should have
a shelter to die in; or,
if you should die on the street,
that you not die cursing others;
or—at long last, the merest crumb of blessing—
that others should not die
cursing you.

II. There's No Crying in Baseball

Lines Written at Twilight on an Intercity Bus

I.

In all the world, there is no place where you are not an interloper.
In every inch of space you travel, on every inch of asphalt you
cross, you trespass. You don't even belong on this bus—both seats
to yourself, what a luxury—that little puddle of light from the
ceiling allowing you to read your H.P. Lovecraft in the failing day.
You've rented the space for a couple of hours. Once the bus stops,
you're through. Your starting point is a dimly remembered dream.
Your destination is a theory. What will be proved once you arrive?

The woman across the aisle from you, nondescript in the semi-
darkness, talks loudly into her cell phone. "Don't blame me!" she
yells. "It's all your fault! It's all your fucking fault!" You look out
the window, at the clouds of rain billowing off the roof of the bus,
obscuring the half-lit city outskirts, and you say to yourself, "Yes,
it *is* my fucking fault."

II.

When the last bus stops running, long after the cars and planes
have gone, where will you be stranded? There are plenty of
possibilities dancing into view. Perhaps the underpass on that dead-
end street. Or that warehouse doused with rust, surrounded by an
empty expanse of cracked concrete, a parking lot for weeds.

Maybe one of the hulks at the roadside, stripped of seats and tires,
will give you shelter. Maybe even the one you're riding now. Glass
from the smashed-out windows will crackle on the gummy floor.
You will stare out at the twilight, at the flat and treeless plain, and
wonder if the lights you see are torches heading toward you. Or if
they come from tarpaper shacks, precious lumps of coal or tallow,
which the people inside, staring at twilight themselves, just might
be willing to share.

A Soaking Rain

This is the sort of rain my father liked: a steady, soaking rain, more than a drizzle but less than a downpour. There was no value to a gullywasher, Dad always said. All that did was wash into the river, and take the topsoil with it. Topsoil was everything; even I knew that. It was Mom, not Dad, who always cited the old quote that all of man's achievements and sophistication were based on six inches of topsoil and the fact that it rains.

Dad grew up on a farm. He wasn't a farmer when he grew up, but those skills helped us all, Mom and my sisters and me. We had four acres of land, stretching back to the river. Even when Dad was working three jobs—driving a sixty-mile mail route, driving a school bus in the morning, working three nights a week as a bartender at the beer joint across the way—he got out the old hand-pushed Gravely and plowed an acre, planting corn and beans, potatoes and tomatoes. He also planted the strawberry patch Mom took care of. We ate well, thanks to Dad. I remember Mom shelling beans and cutting corn off the cob, all from our garden.

It just all seems normal, when you're a kid. You don't really think about how hard your parents work, until you're older. I turned up my nose at the tomatoes and strawberries; I didn't like the seeds. My mom cut corn off the cob because I wouldn't eat it on the cob. I helped plant potatoes, shoving wedges of raw potato into the tilled soil from which new potato vines could grow. I thought my back would give out after half an hour.

When I was a little older, it became my job to weed the strawberry patch. To say I botched the job would be kind. I could barely tell the strawberry plants from the weeds. Soon I lost interest in trying to. Even the jobs I understood, like mowing the lawn, I would mess up by doing things like losing the gas cap on the lawn mower. "Dog *gone* you," Dad would mutter under his breath. He could have said much worse to me, and it would only have been the truth.

When they built the new mall, my dad grieved. "That's some of the best farmland in the county," he said. "It'll never come back. Even if they tear down the mall, it'll be barren forever."

Today we have a steady rain, puddling into whatever soil it can find. It falls on the trunk of my car, which carries the precious bits of corn and tomatoes and strawberries I could ransom at the farmer's market. It falls on the rubble of the failed mall, torn down to make way for something as yet undetermined. It falls on concrete and blacktop and tile, hitting the hard surfaces with a disappointed *smack!,* bashing against the eons it will take the raindrops to burrow through.

Danse D'Enfer

A new dance craze
is sweeping the planet.
It has many names
but only one step,
a forward stomp.
Never backward.
Forward means progress.

In the craze of the crush,
there's only one beat:
the incessant shout of the name
you hate.
The dance floor is paved
with verminous faces
bearing that name.

Shout. Stomp. Repeat.
It's endlessly exciting
and endless: no time
to think or clean up, ever.
Dance shoes are evil
unless washed in blood
in the purifying crush of the craze.

Did I say this was new?
I lied, of course.

Doe at a Street Corner

She waits on the sidewalk as if for a bus. She stands on delicate legs, deciding when to spring. She sniffs the suburban air for predators, those with engines and wheels instead of fangs or guns. She looks both ways. Natural selection: she is not one of those who will die a martyr to the freedom of crossing a road when she pleases, and her fawns will learn this wisdom from her. Her enemies are in hiding, but she has no place to hide. Her enemies have folded into themselves like flowers without sun. They are sparse on the street. They go nowhere; the reasons for them to go anywhere are negated. She has never told where she is going, nor have any of her kind. But now she has fewer places to go, which is why she is here. It is certain she cannot stay. Her ears twitch. The sound of traffic is a faraway drone. Looking again, she trots away, on the correct side of the road. From a power line comes the call of a mourning dove.

A Lesson from a Tooth

You learn the wages of gluttony
for candy and cookies when you are six,
but also the meaning of love:
the one who stays beside you into the night,
placing slivers of ice on a baby tooth,
those shards the only thing between you
and screaming agony.
                              The tooth will be pulled
in the morning, but this is still night.
The shadows on the wall are blobs of pain
contorting with the spasms in your jaw,
and all that spares you are the icy spoon,
the gentle hand and face.

In the rushed journey between six and sixty
you hope you have learned more lessons
than a rotted tooth can teach you,
but above all you hope, through all the shadows,
you have done something one-thousandth as good
as sitting at a bedside through the night,
offering your heart, spoon by spoon.

Conundrum

The third paragraph on page 149 of a book by an author no one has ever heard of, bearing the wrong dust jacket, and shelved in the wrong section of a neglected library in a dreary suburb of a dying city, contains the one truth that, if it could be read by those who would truly understand it, would be the catalyst for every wonderful thing—every conceivable wonderful thing—accruing to everyone in the world.

Those who would understand that truth wait on the steps of that library. It is always winter where they wait. They are hungry and cold, longing for the light and warmth inside. When the doors open, they are repulsed by the smell of musty paper that wafts from inside. Nevertheless, they wag their tails, beseeching all who leave to allow them to enter, or to take them home.

Hopper: *Cape Cod Evening*

at the National Gallery of Art, Washington

Only the dog is alive,
standing alertly in the brown marsh grass,
ears and nose quivering, pointed toward the distance.

The dog is indifferent to the squatting man.
The grudging stretched-out hand is bereft of treats
or anything a waxwork couldn't give.

The cross-armed woman slumps against the window,
straitjacketed in her hard teal dress,
wishing the man, the dog, the world were dead.

The blue spruce forest crowds against the house.
The closest tree lifts a branch against the clapboard,
tasting it, judging if it's time to move.

Grandma and the Hurricane

"The Big Dipper—she's losing!"

The wind is so strong that it blows the constellations around in the sky. Never losing their shape, they are cookie cutters tumbling against each other. A spray of misty stars spills from the Big and Little Dippers, and from the jug of Aquarius. The two fish of Pisces flop helplessly, impaled on the trident of Poseidon. Aries, Taurus and Leo charge Sagittarius, who cannot steady his bow. Canis Minor laughs to see such sport.

Earth, caught in the gale, feels unsteady under your feet. There is only one thing to do: tell Grandma.

You watch the cartoon you running into Grandma's house. The real you stands in her kitchen, warm and smelling of the chicken broth that simmers with her homemade noodles on the old-fashioned stove. She is snapping beans into her battered iron pot, as you have seen her do more times than you can count in your half-decade of life.

Grandma is calm and patient. She always is.

"What is it, honey?" she asks, not looking up from her beans.

You want to say, "GRANDMA, GRANDMA, THERE'S A HURRICANE!" You know that if you say that, everything will be all right.

But the invisible hand reaches from behind and grips your mouth. All you can say is, "Grahh, grahh, therahurrahane!"

Grandma never looks up. She never learns of the danger that only you could warn her of.

And you wake up, in your calm dark bedroom, a gentle breeze playing in the starlight outside your window.

You think of that again, waking not a half-decade but a half-century later, to a howling wind of February. Invisible hands throw fistfuls of stars at your windows. The three-a.m. clouds admit no light; the streetlamps flicker in the storm. You are alone, and you can see Grandma only in your dreams.

The Afterlife of Adolf Hitler

Hitler's morning in the afterlife begins promptly at nine. Cherubs come knocking on the golden door of his high-windowed bedroom, bearing his hot milk, his zwieback, his dark chocolate bar broken into squares just the way he likes it. Fluttering over him like solicitous doves, they dress him in his superbly pressed uniform and high polished boots, so he can strike a truly resolute pose in front of his mirror.

At nine-thirty they lead him to his studio, where his easel stands in the glow of an Alpine sun, the mountains cool and unyielding in the view from his window. His canvas, pure as an Aryan heart, gleams with the pride of knowing that soon it will bear the loftiest inspirations of the Führer. His brushes line up with the precision of an honor guard, and of all his paints, none shines with such burnished glory as the Prussian blue.

Till twelve the Führer stands at his easel, painting a world that only he could envision. Then the cherubs accompany him to the exhibit hall where his greatest creations are shown, and where soon the judging will take place. Hitler stands at a corner of the hall, greeting his admirers with that avuncular dignity so well known to Goebbels and Speer.

At one the results of the judging are announced. It is a different painter every day who makes the announcement; today, it is Camille Pissarro. Monsieur Pissarro steps up to the microphone and makes the same announcement that Edward Hopper made the day before, and Gerard ter Borch the day before that, and that Sandro Botticelli will make the day after, and Edvard Munch the day after that:

"We are pleased to announce the results of the judging. For the best painting in the exhibition, second prize goes to Herr Adolf Hitler, first prize to Mr. Winston Churchill."

A scream rises above the applause. "THIS IS AN OUTRAGE! I AM GREATER THAN WINSTON CHURCHILL! I AM THE GREATEST PAINTER WHO EVER LIVED!"

From the ensuing silence comes a voice, usually that of Goethe or Beethoven: "You are the greatest *house* painter who ever lived."

"THAT IS A LIE! A LIE AND A SLANDER! I WAS *NEVER* A HOUSE PAINTER! IT IS A LIE, I TELL YOU! A LIE OF THE JEWS AND THE AMERICANS!" Turning a color that reaches the subtle midpoint between an eggplant and a boiled lobster, the Führer tears off his own head and hurls it out the window into the street. The window is always closed; the head lands face down in the crash, driving shards of glass into the glacial blue eyes. The headless body lurches out the door, and—having reached a blood pressure of 666 over 490—it explodes.

Watching from the broken window, cheerful with his Cohiba and Courvoisier, the winner of the judging says, "Corporal Schicklgruber should not develop more anger than he can contain."

The severed head, the ragged pieces of flesh and bone and viscera, all pulsate in the street. Children with numbers tattooed on their arms play a pick-up game of soccer with the head. The head flexes its bloody mouth, trying to shriek, but its vocal cords are rent asunder. Packs of dogs, led by Lassie and Rin-Tin-Tin, lick up the blood from the asphalt, gnawing the bones and the meat. Then the children take the dogs home to play. The cherubs scatter, to do whatever cherubs do when not waiting on denizens of the afterlife.

At dawn, after lying in the street all day and all night, the tidbits of Hitler drag themselves back home. Stuttering blood along the pavement, they agonize inch by inch, over dog feces and broken glass, up to the door, up the staircase, into the bedroom. Crawling onto the bed, they bind together painfully, head to neck, limb to torso, joint to joint, until they make what might be considered a man, just in time for the cherubs to knock on the golden door at nine, bearing the hot milk, the zwieback, the dark chocolate bar broken into squares just the way he likes it.

Tom Hanks Was Right

Get this straight: there's no such thing as a happy memory. Memories of happy times are memories of what you've lost, and memories of sad times are memories of how you lost it. Forget memories. That's all there is to it.

You're asking what that has to do with Tom Hanks, and how that makes him right. Well, you remember *A League of Their Own,* don't you? What Tom Hanks said? "THERE'S NO CRYING IN BASEBALL!" He was dead on about that. You think Derek Jeter or A-Rod start bawling when they're called out at home? You think Barry Bonds or Roger Clemens go boo-hoo-hoo when Big Bad Henry Waxman grills them about steroids? That's the point. There's no crying in baseball, and there are no memories in public. You can't start remembering things on the street, or in a restaurant, or on the bus, just like you can't start blubbering when you strike out. People hate that. They fear it. When you start thinking about happy times, you start saying to yourself all the things you said then, and all the things people said to you. When you start thinking about sad times, you start saying the things you wish you'd said then, and the things you wish people had said to you. And there you are. In public. Talking to yourself. They've got places for people like that. Whenever they lock someone up, they breathe a sigh of relief—that is, till one of *them* starts talking to himself and gets shoved in his own rubber room.

So if you're going to start remembering, stop. All you can do is step up to bat and forget about everything except the pitcher who's on the mound right now. Forget about him (or her) as soon as your turn at bat is over. And forget about it if your team loses. Or if it wins.

The Map

A crumbling sheet of paper, wavering lines to mark a road and river, a ragged oval denoting a lake: this was the fishing map you left me. We'd never fished together before, I never even liked to fish, but suddenly it seemed like the best idea in the world. I couldn't come north with you just then, but you left the directions I promised I'd keep safe, for myself and everybody, until we needed them. The lines on the map wiggled like worms on a hook, fading and reappearing, changing and reconfiguring.

When I woke that morning, I drew that map again and again. I added blobs of yellow for sun, stoplight-green triangles for pines, blue blotches for skies and lakes. To draw that map is to draw in crayon. Not to draw the map, to say it is not worth drawing, is to live with a blank page on which you can draw nothing. That is why I draw and redraw what I've only dreamed: the place where we will be together, happier than we ever were down south, with all of the fishermen's catch.

Italian-American

for Sophia and Mario

It was October in Montegufoni.
Steel-jawed crushers wolfed Chianti grapes
in joyous cartfuls, and pomegranates
insinuated purple light from dooryards.
I stood outside the castle, waiting
with the others for the *autobus* to take us
to Florence or Lucca or San Gimignano
when another bus, the color of *sorbetto di limone,*
pulled into view. Small children, taking
no notice of the queued-up Americans,
tumbled out of the bus, clutching soccer balls
and Hello Kitty or Donald Duck lunchboxes,
laughing in a language I did not know.
But I thought of another *bambina* just born
an ocean and a continent away,
her mother—my niece—the same northern mixture
of Irish-English-German-Dutch as me,
her father one generation removed
from Sicily and Abruzzo.

And now I think of *due bambini,*
sister and brother, growing up in a place
where crushers wolf Cabernet and Zinfandel grapes
for Mondavi, Parducci, Sebastiani.
The first time they went to Italy, they wanted
to travel by balloon. The second time,
Pope Francis blessed them at Easter Mass.
They're renowned from Pescara to Santa Rosa,
these mighty swimmers and marathon readers,
heroes of Golden State soccer fields,
fans of Team Italia, growers of pomegranates.

Elvis and Di's Nuptials in Heaven

Elvis Presley and Princess Diana were married in the Cathedral of Heaven, before 800 million of their most intimate friends, on what would have been last Wednesday at 3:30 p.m. if they had still been in linear time.

The cathedral was at its most magnificent; the designer of the Hanging Gardens of Babylon outdid himself, festooning the nave with truckloads of every non-carnivorous flower known on every inhabited planet in the Universe, in ways that enhanced the artworks by Leonardo, Michelangelo, Raphael, Botticelli, Tintoretto, Giotto, Titian, Donatello, Cellini, Del Sarto, Fra Angelico, Fra Lippo Lippi, Filippino Lippi, and even Caravaggio, who received a day pass from Hell to do a quick mural.

To the tune of Johann Sebastian Bach's organ prelude, which he composed expressly for the occasion, the fashionable guests were shown to their seats by ushers James Dean, Jim Morrison, and Jimi Hendrix. JFK and Jackie were the best man and matron of honor, and lovely in pink were the bridesmaids—Marilyn Monroe, Audrey Hepburn, and Mother Teresa. ("Teresa darling, you look almost like a man," said guest Noel Coward. "So do you, Noel," Teresa quipped back.)

The bride and groom were resplendent in their diamond-, ruby- and emerald-encrusted matching jumpsuits, designed by Gianni Versace himself and made from the finest tanned skins of Andrew Cunanan. Henry VIII, demanding pride of place among British royalty, obtained a day pass from Hell to give the bride away before the Reverend Doctor Martin Luther King, Jr. The bride and groom recited their vows to each other, written for them for the occasion by Shakespeare, Lord Byron, Kahlil Gibran, Charles Bukowski, and Kurt Cobain. Bach played variations on "Love Me Tender" as the couple exchanged their first kiss as man and wife, and a hundred thousand cherubs flew around the nave, carrying banners bearing messages of good luck to the new couple, in 24-karat gold lamé, in 297 different languages including 56 extinct and 14 "speaking in tongues."

After the wedding the guests were treated to a sumptuous buffet prepared by Vatel, Carême, Escoffier, and Ho Chi Minh, although to Elvis' chagrin they balked at the deep-fried peanut butter-and-banana appetizers he wanted. Emily Dickinson caught the bridal bouquet, and Peter Abelard the garter. The band, led by John Lennon, included George Harrison, Roy Orbison, Buddy Holly, Ritchie Valens, the Big Bopper, Janis Joplin, Stevie Ray Vaughan, Frank Zappa, Keith Moon, Jerry Garcia, Muddy Waters, Robert Johnson, Louis Armstrong, Duke Ellington, Count Basie, Charlie Parker, John Coltrane, Miles Davis, Charles Mingus, Gene Krupa, Benny Goodman, Hank Williams, Patsy Cline, Johnny & June Carter Cash, Frank Sinatra, Ella Fitzgerald, Billie Holiday, Hildegard von Bingen, Dvorak, Sibelius, Stravinsky, Tchaikovsky, Shostakovich, Rachmaninov, and Mozart. Nixon and Mao made a smash hit with the crowd when they danced naked to "Whatever Gets You Through the Night." (That's the only work for which Nixon and Mao can get day passes from Hell these days—dancing naked at John Lennon's gigs.)

Andy Warhol took the wedding pictures, a process that went more smoothly after Ansel Adams reminded Andy to take the cap off the lens. When the 2,806,184-tiered cake was cut, Di playfully tried to smash the first piece into Elvis' face; Elvis ducked, and Di shoved the cake right in the kisser of Alexander the Great. Everyone laughed, none louder than Aristotle. ("That makes up for a *lot* of math homework that was never turned in!" Aristotle whispered to Schopenhauer, who grunted his approval.) There were a few unpleasant moments, as there are at every wedding: Jackie elbowed JFK in the ribs when she caught him looking a little too intently at Marilyn, and a drunken brawl threatened to break out between Ernest Hemingway and Christopher Marlowe, which fortunately was nipped in the bud when Jack Johnson and Daniel Boone restrained them.

But of course the magic moment came when Elvis sang "Love Me Tender" directly to Di, accompanied by the Jordanaires and a choir of ten thousand seraphim. As the love light in Elvis' eyes met the love light in Di's, the Milky Way Galaxy ignited with the Aurora Borealis, spreading light across the sky in 1,907 subtle yet bold gradations of 146 different hues, so that the heavens glittered for hours, days, and eons.

As Oscar Wilde opined for the *Elysian Times Literary Supplement,* "The display was fireworks of an intensely spiritual nature, beautiful and perfect, as the princess and the troubadour demonstrated for eternity the triumph of optimism over experience." Isaac Newton and Albert Einstein presented opposing theories of the celestial phenomenon for the journal *Scientific Heaven.* Hedda Hopper—who got a day pass from Hell to report on the doings for the Cerberus News Network—said, "It was to `Di' for!"

And who among you would call me a liar, or a blasphemer? I swear to you all I have said is true—as true as the faint rim of violet that lingers over the hills after a sunset, as the memory of spring daffodils after they have withered in summer's heat, as the wind you thought you felt ruffling your hair as you walked outside your door.

His Face

Did you take the wrong vitamins? Eat the wrong things? Did you exercise too little? What nourishment did you lack, what deficiency do you have, that seeing this face, nearly forgotten after forty years, should make you feel as if your heart had been slashed out?

He wasn't even anyone you knew. He was a shadow always, an image on a screen. He went away, you went on. Then, suddenly, on the edge of the cable channel list, there he is again, honey-haired and limpid-eyed, a sweet and beautiful boy. Nations have vanished, continents are in flames, the polar ice cap is lukewarm salt water. Yet he is the same as he always was. And so are you.

You are used to growing old, and to others growing old. But this face is not old, will never be old. Somewhere there is a man, gray-haired or bald, who once was this boy. You will never see that man. He is not dead; the Internet tells you as much. You are not dead; the mirror tells you as much.

The yawning ache grows worse, demanding food that does not exist. The mirror and the screen are the same: ice floes, cold, empty, and flat. There is nothing to sustain you, nothing to learn, nothing to turn to—only that face, which will not go away, creating a void that allows nothing to fill it.

Monkey with a Piece of Cucumber

Now you are tired—tired even of flinging the damn things out of your cage. They have started piling up, little gray-green corpses stinking up the place. You pick one up: a slimy chunk of nothing.

You pulled the strings and pushed the buttons just as well, just as quickly and enterprisingly, as the monkey in the cage beside you. He does not even deign to look at you. He fondles his purple jewel of grape, so delicate, so opalescent, so much more delicious than a hunk of cucumber. He glories in the moment just before he devours it, basking in his worthiness to possess it.

He does not look at the humans outside. You do. They slice cucumbers thinly for tea sandwiches, make luscious sour tzatziki, gorge on every color of grape, dry them into raisins, crush them into wine, fizz them into champagne, stomp on them just for the hell of it because they have so damn many.

The monkey in the next cage closes his eyes, congratulating himself. His cage is bare, because he eats his grapes as he gets them. There will be no more till tomorrow. He does not seem to know this.

You look at the rotting thing you hold. It dissolves into putrid pulp, slipping out of your fingers.

For the first time, you realize you have hands.

.

III. To Live Completely and a Thousandfold

Man on Terrace with Wine, Recalling a Line from Hermann Hesse

What happiness to dream when, drinking wine,
You notice beauty that you never see
When sober and at work. Late summer vines
Glisten with purple fruit. Serenity

Drifts through the willows, buoys the scent and sight
Of lavender and baked earth. Tenderness
Wafts from the hills and permeates the light.
You get it by the bottle or the glass.

You can't prolong this feeling, yet you must.
If only life itself could be your wine!
You feel not dulled, but heightened. Even dust,
Waltzing in sunlit motes, seems rich and fine,

And you feel you are better than yourself.
The mountains are your friends, the grass your home.
Why must this soaring pleasure be so brief
That, sooner than you've reached your car, it's gone?

Birds hop on empty tables, pecking crumbs
And tipping beaks into abandoned dregs.
Vineyards and flagstones steep in Napa sun—
A benediction, bright and plain. You beg

To live completely and a thousandfold.
Where are the vineyards when the way is rough?
If, deep inside you, there's a place to hold
A drop of stillness, will it be enough?

It Was Over So Fast

like one of the shorter
fugues from *Das Wohltempierte Klavier*—
but you were distracted
and missed the first notes;
the rhythm skittered senselessly away.
Just as you caught up
with the commingled voices
and you realized this
was something that nourished you—
music to love, and even to live by—
it stopped.

A Mother Waits

He always was a good boy: sensitive,
Stubborn perhaps, not diligent in class,
But with an artist's soul. What I would give
To see him aid the priest once more at Mass,

Swinging the censer with devotion. He
Was grave and handsome as he served the Host
And lit the altar tapers. Faithfully
He praised the Father, Son, and Holy Ghost.

He looked so thin and lonely on the train
To art school and—he hoped—to fame. But why
In failure did he choose to stay where rain
Fell on the city's poor as from God's eye?

When I grew ill, he came back to my side,
His tears cascading in the oil lamp's shine.
I begged him to be strong before I died,
And I caressed his face—a mirror of mine.

Gaunt, ragged, barefoot, the new ones come through
With numbers on their arms. From my cold place
I ask them of my son. Christian or Jew,
They stare in horror. Some spit in my face.

More years than I can count, I've had to wait.
Why do they treat me so? What have I done
That I should be regarded with such hate?
And why will no one tell me of my son?

Poetry and Music

He hoists ungrateful bricks up decorative ladders
too dainty for the weight.
Over millennia, his fathers and mothers
molded bricks into arabesques,
Grecian statues, free-form improvisations.
He knows the rules, those tacky globs
of mortar, but the secret of melting bricks
is something no one can teach or learn.
He looks at his hands. He looks at the bricks.
Dull red, unpliable, they look
defiantly like what they mean.

She tries to dam the stream using only her hands.
Over millennia, her fathers and mothers
solidified water between their fingers,
built palaces, cathedrals, pyramids.
Their secret can't be taught or learned.
Their rules are crows on telephone wires,
scattering at their own discord.
She could wait for winter, but ice
is slippery, dissolving at first sun.
She looks at her hands. She looks at the water
bathing her hands, the stream-bed pebbles
in dull mosaic, the cloisonné fish
eluding her grasp. The ceaseless
water-sound and crows' caws mingle,
signifying—what?

They toil side by side,
too busy to notice each other
till he drops a brick in the stream.
She looks up. He looks down.
His eyes trace arabesques.
Her eyes build cathedrals.
The brick bends. The water stops.
From somewhere, a faint sound mimics birdsong.

Poem of Ecstasy

It is just before the light seeps in,
and the radio has been on all night.
The host announces the next selection,
Scriabin's *Poem of Ecstasy,*
which you have never heard before,
and the station has never played before.
The music is formless layers of smoke
billowing from far underground.
You see the gunmetal gray miasma
and smell the world on fire.

You like to leave the radio on
all night. You like to have
those great purveyors of tapestries—
Bach, Mozart, Beethoven, Brahms—
unfurl their wares in front of you,
weaving them into your dreams.
Tonight, however, it did not work.
The music was only the chittering
of zoetrope fiends on your bedroom wall.

You hugged yourself in the dark,
knowing the shadows would be real by morning.
You thought please don't let the light come
oh god please no light

And then—light.
Scriabin's conflagration
ends on a triumphant chord
that does not seem to fit the music.
The sky-blue-pink of a sunny dawn
butters the room. The radio,
serene as Wilhelm Kempff's piano,
plays "Sheep May Safely Graze."

A Vandalized Churchyard

The headstones that withstood
A thousand storms and snows
Slant broken in the mud
Like fallen dominoes.
And that's the way it goes.

Why should we make a fuss
About some shattered stone?
To be anonymous,
Unheeded and alone
Is the one truth we've known,

So do the dead deserve
The dignity of name?
Time throws all life a curve;
It's just a children's game,
From age to age the same.

Children must have play
Before they go to bed.
They run an ancient way—
Where those now ashes led—
To unname all the dead.

Cornflowers

Stippling the flanks of cracked concrete,
The violet-blue of daydreamed skies
Grows from the earth as rooted eyes
   Where road and farmland meet.

They keep watch on each passing car,
Bobbing and ducking in the breeze
That blasts from monster SUVs
   And smells of melted tar.

The insect-carapaced parade
Streaks past in steel monotony.
The children of velocity,
   Their journeys factory-made,

May see what waves like tiny fans
Around them, lined against the wind—
Dream-colored, staring, left behind
   With tossed-out soda cans.

To Avoid Paris

Plow through the forest; spare no owl or tree.
The Third Estate can never spoil your plans.
With axes, paving stones and peasantry
You can be just as bold as Louis Quinze

Who, when Parisians rudely asked him why
Their sons were being shanghaied to Quebec,
Built roads to Fontainebleau straight from Versailles
So he could keep impertinence in check.

The Louvre's not worth it, or the *haute cuisine.*
Speed past the outskirts with your curtains drawn.
It's better to be king than to be seen.
Lay waste to everything you must. Drive on.

Alan Arkin Wins the Steak Knives

Some days I blunder into so much pain,
The urge to win ensuring every loss,
That in my dreams I wish I had the faith
Of Alan Arkin in *Glengarry Glen Ross,*

Who, speaking softly, has no stick at all,
But keeps his head down and averts his eye
Making sales calls no one wants to hear
To people who cannot afford to buy.

He never dreams of first-place Cadillacs—
Everyone knows that's Al Pacino's due—
But prays third-place dismissal will not be
His fate, as Alec Baldwin shouts, "FUCK YOU!"

Jack Lemmon and Ed Harris curse at life,
Hash out long-faded triumphs over beers
And plot the theft of Mitch and Murray's leads
As Kevin Spacey, sneering, overhears...

But Alan Arkin, neither newly wheeled
Nor cuffed and printed, always lives to take
The latest set of steak knives gratefully
In faith that, one fine day, there will be steak.

To an Obscure Vegetable

Kohlrabi, rutabaga,
whatever your name,
you squat in the produce bin against the wall,
banished as far as possible
from the sunniness of clementines
and the evergreen of broccoli.

People skew their noses
at your knobby purple-grayness.
Not even a Niagara Falls of cheese sauce
could barrel you down a child's gullet,
and you have no place in the leafy salads
lithe women in leotards fling into bowls
on the run to Pilates class.

It takes the silent man
who wanders unseen by housewives and stockboys
to hold you in his hand,
survey your deformities
and nod at all the secret truths you bear.
With a chant of ginger
and a prayer of cilantro
he will slice you to your roots
and steam you pure,
revealing at last what you hold within you—
something of value, something of earth.

Shadow of a Doubt: Charles Oakley's Speech

Santa Rosa Ladies' Club, 1943

Good ladies, thanks for asking me to speak.
Though Emma gave my arm a friendly twist
To get me to accept, I see her point.
I would have been a blackguard and a churl
To turn down such a lovely group as you.
It is a joy to be in Santa Rosa—
This vine-embroidered gem of California,
Fair city of the Valley of the Moon
Whose beauty rivals even Tuscany's.
You've much to cherish here, and though I know
You come from hardy Forty-Niner stock,
Like all Americans, you wonder how
You can protect the freedom you hold dear
From Hitler, Tojo, and their death-crazed hordes.
Of course you know that if I had the answers,
I'd be at Mr. Roosevelt's side right now!
But I can say this much: We built this land
With courage and with hope, so when we face
A peril such as this, we'll stand our ground;
Shoulder to shoulder, we will fight and win.
We won at Yorktown and at Appomattox,
We won at San Juan Hill and Belleau Wood.
In times of crisis, we endure and thrive.
Don't think Pearl Harbor will go unavenged!

(Applaud, you morons. Clap your trotters, swine.
Powder your snouts and swill your rubber chicken
And grunt with pleasure at my flattery.
Good night, fair sows. Regain your squalid sties
And wallow in your stinking excrement.
I'd shove you all in Hitler's cattle cars
If he weren't of the same foul stuff as you.

68

Tomorrow you will hail me on the street
And smile and wave and shake your silly jewels—
The jewels that, soon enough, I'll turn to cash.
How happily you'll greet your murderer.
When rid of you, I will endure and thrive.
Don't think my anguish will go unavenged.)

Nursery Rhyme

When horses swim with killer whales
   And water's made of wood,
When hills are weighed on bathroom scales,
   That's when we'll all be good.

When morning rises from the west
   And harvest moons are banned,
When wolves hatch from a pigeon's nest,
   That's when we'll understand.

When rabbits go with grave intent
   To seek out common ends
Before the Raptor Parliament,
   That's when we'll all be friends.

When Tweets and iPhones grow on trees
   And men no longer grease
Their guns with blood from enemies,
   That's when we'll all have peace.

Infanticide

Revising poetry is like killing your babies.
                              —Dorothy Parker

You hone the point and pray it's for the best.
The cradle shudders from a feral cry.
You raise the pen above your baby's chest.

Let's face it now: you never have been blessed
With children born as right as apple pie.
You hone the point and pray. It's for the best,

This little operation. You have messed
Before with babies ugly, bent, awry.
You raise the pen above your baby's chest,

Its flared proboscis in its armpit nest,
Its fangs, five ears and one magenta eye.
You hone the point and...
                              Pray it's for the best,

You makeshift Doctor Frankenstein, confessed
Creator of monstrosities! On high
You raise the pen. Above your heaving chest

Your brainpan's giddy from this final test:
Whether this child—and you—will live or die.
You hone the point and pray it's for the best.
You raise the pen above your baby's chest.

71

Shadow Dancing

A four-year-old is dancing with herself.
In the midsummer sun, she paints arabesques,
the lawn her canvas, her body her brush.
She has known all her life how to make her own fun,
how to be her own friend,
but this is something new:
those endless patterns she alone creates
with her arms and legs, changing every second,
extend with the lengthening afternoon light
past the end of her yard, to all her neighbors.

And how long, seriously, can she dance?
What's fun at four may pall at forty,
or even at five. And what if she dances
past four? Not everybody fits
in toe shoes, or bends properly at the barre—
the price of importuning the world with dance.
We've all seen untrained dancers swaying
to music they alone can hear
at street corners, bus stops, subway stations,
and all we want is for them to dance
locked away from us, where we cannot see.

But, for this living moment, let her dance.
She has all her life to socialize her art.
Let her prance and sway as she pleases, or stop
to stretch her arms toward the sun,
the shadow of her childlike reach extending
past the end of her yard, to all the world.

To a Modern Poet

With shards of words as dissonant as truck
Gears grinding, you assert you cannot live
Without Beethoven, Mozart, Schubert, Bach,
And other courtly music. Yet you give
The bird to courtly verse. When you see rhymes
And meters, you're affronted by the thought
Of this assault on modern art and times.
Sonatas you esteem, but sonnets not.
So why should avant-garde posterity
Reward your cursed contrariness of rage?
To cure your foolish inconsistency,
We must replace your music with John Cage,
Carl Ruggles, Milton Babbitt, and George Crumb.
May you absorb their clinkers till you're numb.

To a Bee

At your right wing's my open backyard door
And safety; at your left, my upraised shoe.
The choice of life or death is amply clear,
So how then can you *not* know what to do?
You zigzag and you pause, you feint and hover
Around my kitchen walls bereft of pollen;
Are you so keen to have your name forever
Carved on the monument to your hive's fallen?

Is it a whiff of roses from outside
That penetrates your milligram of mind
To make you beat your simple wings and ride
The air to freedom, leaving doom behind?
Go have your summer, little jackanapes!
May you have many more hair's-breadth escapes.

A War of Two Words

"Delphinium" seems to have won its war
With "larkspur." Who could doubt its victory?
A word that's such an elephantine bore,
Borne of botanical authority,
Will always win against a graceful sound
That lilts but lacks the proper stately weight.
The blooms are rooted in the solid ground—
Flowers of destiny, and not of fate.
So "larkspur" goes away—a summer word
As evanescent as the butterfly
You saw just now; as fleeting as the bird
Ascending swiftly in the cloudless sky
Above the rose-drenched garden you just passed—
A vision that was never meant to last.

Nothing Stops

Along the street, it cartwheels into sight
In stiff October wind. Dime-flat and gray
As bus exhaust, is it a baby's kite
Or someone's fast-food box from yesterday?
You only know that tires worked overtime
To fashion such a wafer. In a whirl
Of waltzing leaves and sparkling front-porch chime,
You see it closely: oh my God, a *squirrel!*

And nothing stops. A guy in denim yawns,
Strides past, looks at his watch. A leaf blower roars
Its thoughtless lust for leaves across the lawns.

Great oaks will grow from the forgotten stores
Of this cadaver in full autumn sail,
Still ruddered by a froufrou fluff of tail.

Watching Godzilla in 3D

This is your painless dose of shock and awe:
A mile of scaled and sinewed CGI
Arising from a pixel sea. Each claw
And fang engulfs the conflagrating sky.
Tokyo, Las Vegas, San Francisco crumble
In tune to Dolby's all-surrounding roar
As you applaud the glass and stone that tumble
Down from the screen and vanish toward the floor.

You're CGI yourself. On cue you smile
With all the film's insipid hireling crowd
At this tyrannosaurus-crocodile
Whose gaze you're primed to say is brave and proud,
That stomps back to its ocean, having killed
A world you didn't make, and can't rebuild.

Return of the King

The pigeon towers in his pride of place—
An outdoor table, Hampton Court Café.
Big as a hen, he thrusts his blunt-beaked face
Into a tourist's unattended tray
Of crisps and sausage rolls. His wrathful gaze
Warns anyone who might usurp his prize;
He seems to ponder all his past-life ways
Of cutting wives and traitors down to size.
From a safe distance, his winged subjects coo
Their *Vivat Rex!* from crenellated towers
Above the ancient clock that heaved its two
Strong hands to count five hundred years of hours—
Hours that saw castles, kings, and countries burn—
And chimes *Te Deum* for the king's return.

Jack Horner's Sonnet

The corner's fine if you don't have to stand.
It's clean, well-lighted, with a comfy chair
And Christmas pies profusely close at hand.
You'd be surprised how well you'd like it there!
Before you, two strong walls serenely meet;
Above, below, the trim of beveled wood.
Monotonous, perhaps, but what a treat
That all you've seen, you've surely understood.
No work, no sorrow, just a steady calm
In contemplation of a crust and plums.
No need for even a vestigial qualm
Occasioned by the pricking of your thumbs
Or all the screams behind you, sirens, noise.
I am the luckiest and best of boys.

Death of a Barber

The woman in the smock hacks at my hairy
Scalp with her scissors as the daylight fades.
"A heart attack—he went so fast. Poor Larry,"
She says with all the warmth of her steel blades.
A magazine from June 2002
Lies dogeared in an empty chair. The shears
Snap briskly to the swish of rinsed shampoo.
My disembodied hair drifts down like years.

The strip mall's lights begin their nightly glow.
Across the street, the Pilgrim Holiness
Church's neon sign blares JESUS SAVES.
The streams of peacock efflorescence flow
In waves along an orphaned patch of grass—
What Whitman called the uncut hair of graves.

An Oldie

That song you used to love begins to play
On FM radio. The plaintive fiddle
Lilts in your ears in that cathartic way
It always did.
              It stinks then, how the middle
Devolves into a synthesizer slog
With lyrics of a baby-babbling kind.
It kills you, what a monumental dog
This song is. But you never used to mind.
The tune, the violin still cancels all
Your fine discernment and unerring taste.
Marked as a sentimental fool, you crawl
Toward your exacting mind, a heart debased
By all the tawdry dives it used to haunt.
How we betray ourselves by what we want.

The Church Dance

Greeley, Colorado, 1949

After the cake and punch, the lights grow dim.
The pastor's phonograph purrs "String of Pearls."
Young bodies swaying softly to that hymn
Of love press close together, boys and girls
Fresh from the ranch house looking for their fun.
Angels in dungarees and gingham, bright
With God's own joy, dance slowly one on one,
Suspended in the starry Western night.

But in a corner chair a lonely man
Hears demons chant, sees libertine and bawd
Cut capers roughshod, grunt like swine, and fan
Their quivering buttocks in the face of God.
He vows in Allah's name that, from this day,
These infidels and all their spawn must pay.

How to Survive

You cower in a corner of the room—
Eternal refuge of the gray and small.
If you stay hidden, you can stave off doom
By edging past the bottom of the wall.
You move in darkness, and your mind is numb
From hearing others perish snap by snap.
This is what life and pleasure have become:
A blob of peanut butter in a trap.
If you eat only crumbs, and make no noise,
And seek no company, and shun all light;
If you are wise enough to know that joys
Are not for you, and neither is a fight—
You might escape all those who find you vile
And live another unimportant while.

The Art of Fugue

Fuga a 3 Soggetti (Contrapunctus XIV),
left unfinished at Bach's death

Eight notes diffusing softly into space
From Bach's last fugue go dangling, spiraled, broken—
A universe of counterpoint unspoken,
Forever incomplete and in a place
To which Bach left no map.
                      Time can't erase
These notes or make them whole, although their oaken
Resonance might be for some a token
Of rocklike certainty in Christian grace—
A fugue to finish at the throne of God.
For others, it might mean the simple end,
The proof that all lives come to nothingness.
These pensive notes resound, these notes we prod
With instruments to try to comprehend
A place whose landscape we can only guess.

A Modern Nativity

A noise at midnight in my garden shed
Drove the dog nuts. We stumbled out to see
A newborn baby sleeping peacefully
Inside a rag-stuffed wheelbarrow bed.
His mom and daddy stared at me with dread—
Two shabby working folks society
Cut loose. The single light bulb, hanging free,
Gathered a glow around the baby's head.

What happened next? I'm not sure I can say.
I can't describe just how I felt, or feel.
I heard a voice intoning, "You can stay."
It offered them some blankets and a meal.
The dog stopped barking, which is not his way.
I had no earthly clue a dog could kneel.

Drink Up

*...as bright and full of promise as moonlight
in a martini.*
      —John Patrick Shanley, *Moonstruck*

Heaven is yours inside a tall stemmed glass,
An Eiffel Tower inverted on its tail.
A million opportunities may pass;
This is the one to grab, this Holy Grail,
This glass of moonlight shining in the dark,
Bright as a Bombay sapphire. Like the eyes
Of new-found lovers, its prismatic spark
Halos the room as if to canonize
The speared and tonsured olive.
                             Never mind
That maybe you have had this drink before.
You threw up, saw pink hippos, staggered blind;
The angry barkeep bounced you out the door.
Never let on you really wanted beer;
This is your chance. Drink up, while it's still here.

About the Author

Miles David Moore was born in Lancaster, Ohio, and received a journalism degree from Ohio University. From 1977 until his retirement in 2020, he was a reporter for Crain Communications Inc. Since 2006 he has been film reviewer for the online arts magazine *Scene4*. In 1994, he founded the IOTA poetry reading series in Arlington, Va., which he hosted until its end in 2017. From 2002 to 2009, he was a member of the board of directors of The Word Works; earlier, he served as administrator of its Washington Prize. In 2016, he received an award from the Arlington Arts Council for his services to poetry. His previous books of poetry are *The Bears of Paris* (Word Works, 1995); *Buddha Isn't Laughing* (Argonne House Press, 1999); and *Rollercoaster* (Word Works, 2004).

www.ingramcontent.com/pod-product-compliance
Lightning Source LLC
Chambersburg PA
CBHW022015080426
42733CB00007B/607